Making Water Kefir

A Complete Guide to Making Your Own Kefir Grains and Tasty Probiotic Drinks

Lucy Potter

copyright@2024 Lucy Potter all right reserved. No part of this publication should be reproduced in any form or means without prior written permission from the copy right holder

Chapter One 5
Making Water Kefir 5

Chapter Two 8
Health Benefits of Probiotics. 8

Chapter Three 16
How fermentation works and why it's good for you 16

Chapter Four 23
Composition and function of water kefir Grains 23

Chapter Six 30
Important Things You Need to Make Water Kefir 30

Chapter Seven 38
Picking the Right Water: Why Water Quality Is Important 38

Chapter Eight 45
A Step-by-Step Guide How to Get Dried Water Kefir Grains 45

Chapter Nine 52
Simple Recipe: Step-by-Step Instructions for Making Water Kefir What You Need: 52

Chapter Ten 60

Adding flavor to your water kefir: Adding herbs, fruits, and other tastes......................60

Chapter One

Making Water Kefir
What are probiotics?

• Probiotics are living microorganisms, most often bacteria and yeasts that are good for your health when you eat enough of them. People often call them "good" or "friendly" germs.

•**Types:** Lactobacillus, Bifidobacterium, and Saccharomyces boulardii are some common types of probiotic strains. Each strain is good for you in different ways and does different things in your body.

- **Sources:** You can find probiotics in yogurt, kefir, sauerkraut, kimchi, miso, and other fermented foods, as well as in nutrition supplements.

What Science Says About Probiotics

- **How Probiotics Work:** Probiotics help keep the balance of bacteria in the gut healthy by stopping the growth of bad bacteria and encouraging the growth of good bacteria. They also help the gut barrier do its job.

- **The Gut Microbiome:** this is made up of trillions of microorganisms that live in the digestive system. For good health, the microbiome needs to be broad and well-balanced.

- **Interaction with the Immune System:** Probiotics boost the immune system by making more natural antibodies and making some immune cells work better.

Chapter Two

Health Benefits of Probiotics.

- **Digestive Health:** Probiotics can help with stomach problems like gas, bloating, diarrhea, and constipation. Also, they can help you deal with conditions like inflammatory bowel disease (IBD) and irritable bowel syndrome (IBS).

- **Immune Support:** Probiotics help lower the risk of getting sick by making the immune system stronger. They make the body's natural defenses against germs stronger.

- **Mental Health:** The gut-brain axis connects the gut to the brain and lets them talk to each other. By changing the production of neurotransmitters and lowering inflammation, probiotics can have a good effect on mood, anxiety, and depression.

• **Skin Health:** Probiotics may help skin problems like acne, eczema, and rosacea by lowering inflammation and giving skin a healthy buffer.

• **General Health:** Probiotics improve general health by making it easier for the body to absorb nutrients, helping with weight loss, making the metabolism healthier, and giving you more energy.

Compare to Kombucha and Milk Kefir, Two Other Fermented Drinks

Water Kefir

• **Base ingredients:** Sugar water or coconut water for the base.

• **Fermentation Process:** This step uses water kefir grains, which are made up of yeasts and bacteria.

• **Taste:** Not too sweet, a little sour, and a little carbonated. Adding herbs or veggies can change the taste.

Probiotic Content: It has a number of good bacteria and

yeasts in it, though not as many types as milk kefir.

- **Nutritional Benefits:** it's full of probiotics, enzymes, and some B vitamins. It has fewer calories and sugar than kombucha.

- **Suitability:** This is a great choice for people who can't have cheese or who want something without caffeine.

kombucha

- **Ingredients:** For the base, you need sweetened tea, usually black or green tea.

- **Fermentation Process:** A SCOBY (Symbiotic Culture of

Bacteria and Yeast) turns the tea into alcohol.

• **Taste:** sour and tangy, with different amounts of sweetness and carbonation. Often made with spices and veggies.

- **Probiotic Content:** It has many good bacteria and yeasts in it, but the kinds can be very different.

• **Nutritional Benefits:** it's full of probiotics, vitamins from tea, and organic acids like acetic acid. It has sugar and caffeine in it, but most of the sugar is used up during brewing.

- **Suitability:** This drink is great for people who like sour, fizzy drinks and want the antioxidants that tea has to offer.

Kefir Milk

- **Base Ingredients:** Milk (from cows, goats, sheep, or non-dairy sources).

- **Fermentation Process:** This step uses milk kefir grains, which are made up of yeasts and bacteria.

- **It tastes creamy,** spicy, and a little sour. Water kefir and kombucha may not be as thick as this one.

- **Probiotics Contents:** There are a lot of different kinds of probiotic strains in this drink, often more than in water kefir or kombucha.

- **Nutritional Benefits:** it's full of minerals, vitamins (B and K), probiotics, proteins, and calcium. Less lactose in the milk can make it easier to digest during fermenting.

- **Suitability:** This is the best drink for people who eat dairy and want a smooth one that is high in probiotics. Versions without dairy can be made for people who can't handle lactose or are allergic to dairy.

Summary

• Water Kefir is a light, refreshing, and flexible probiotic drink that is great for people who don't want to drink dairy or coffee.

• Kombucha is a sour tea-based drink that has the extra health benefits of tea antioxidants. However, it does have some sugar and caffeine in it.

• Milk kefir is the best choice for people who eat dairy because it is smooth, full of nutrients, and has the widest range of probiotics.

Chapter Three

How fermentation works and why it's good for you
How to Ferment

1. How fermentation works:

• Microorganisms, such as bacteria, yeasts, and fungi, turn organic substances, like sugars and carbohydrates, into alcohol or acids during fermentation.

• This process takes place in a place that doesn't have air.

2. Different Ways to Ferment:

• Lactic acid fermentation is the process by which bacteria like Lactobacillus turn sugars into lactic acid. Often found in kimchi, yogurt, and cabbage.

• Yeasts, like Saccharomyces cerevisiae, turn sugars into alcohol and carbon dioxide during the alcohol fermentation process. It is used to bake bread, make wine, and brew beer.

• Acetic Acid Fermentation: Acetobacter bacteria turn alcohol into acetic acid, which is then used to make vinegar.

3. Steps in the fermentation process:

• The bacteria are introduced to the substrate, like kefir grains being added to sugar water.

• The first stage of growth: microorganisms start to eat sugars and grow.

• Active Fermentation: Sugars are quickly changed into acids, gases, or alcohol. Signs that can be seen include bubbles and changes in the way things feel or smell.

• Maturation: As fermentation slows down and microbes settle down, the product develops more complex flavors.

4. Environment Factors:

• Temperature: The best temperatures for fermentation depend on the bacteria, but for lacto-fermentation they are usually between 60°F and 75°F (15°C and 24°C) and for yeast fermentation they are between 68°F and 77°F (20°C and 25°C).

• pH Levels: When food ferments, the pH drops, making the surroundings acidic. This keeps the food fresh and stops harmful bacteria from growing.

Why fermentation is Beneficial

1 .Better nutritional profile:

• Fermentation makes nutrients more bio-available, which means the body can use them more easily. For instance, fermentation can make more of some amino acids, B vitamins, and vitamin K.

• It can also lower anti-nutrients, which are things like phytates in grains that stop the body from absorbing nutrients.

2. Probiotics:

• Fermented foods have a lot of probiotics, which are good bugs that help keep your gut healthy. A good gut microbiome is linked to better mental health, better digestion, and stronger immune systems.

• Probiotics can help keep the gut flora in balance, which stops dangerous bacteria from growing too much.

3. Good Digestive Health:

- Complex carbohydrates, proteins, and fats are broken down during fermentation, which makes food easier to stomach. For example, lacto-fermentation breaks down lactose, which can help people who can't handle lactose.

4. Natural Preservation:

- The fermentation process creates an acidic environment that stops germs and molds that cause food to go bad from growing. This naturally keeps the food fresh without the need for artificial preservatives.

- This makes fermented foods last longer on the shelf.

5. How it tastes and feels:

- Fermentation gives foods and drinks more complicated flavors and a better texture. This method can improve the taste of foods by giving them more tanginess, fizz, and depth.

6. Security:

- During fermentation, acids and alcohols are made, which makes the climate unfriendly to pathogens. This helps to reduce the risk of getting ill from food.

Chapter Four

Composition and function of water kefir Grains

Composition of water kefir grains

1. Structure:

• Water kefir grains are tiny, clear, rubbery structures that look like groups of very small crystals. They are made up of a mesh of bacteria and yeasts that work together (SCOBY).

2. Microbes Community:

• The main types of bacteria found in water kefir grains are Lactobacillus, Leuconostoc, and Acetobacter. These bacteria cause lactic acid fermentation, which makes lactic acid. Lactic acid adds to the sour taste and helps the food stay fresh.

• Yeasts: Saccharomyces, Candida, and Pichia are some of the most common yeasts found in water kefir grains. These yeasts are what make booze by fermenting sugars into ethanol and carbon dioxide, which helps the beer bubble.

3. Polysaccharides:

• The grains stay together because of polysaccharides like dextran, which are made by bacteria in the grains. The polysaccharide matrix gives the grains shape and rigidity.

Function of water kefir grains

1. How fermentation works:

• Sugar Metabolism: When water kefir grains are added to a sugary drink, the bacteria and yeasts in them break down the sugars (sucrose, glucose, and fructose) and make helpful byproducts like lactic acid, ethanol, acetic acid, and carbon dioxide.

• Symbiotic Relationship: Bacteria and yeasts live together and help each other. Bacteria break down sugars into simpler compounds, and yeasts use some of these compounds for further metabolism. This keeps the environment balanced.

2. Making probiotics:

• Different kinds of good bacteria and yeasts are made during fermentation. These probiotics can help keep the microbiome in your gut in order, make digestion better, and make your immune system stronger.

3. Taste and carbonation:

• The unique taste of water kefir comes from the metabolic activities of the bacteria and yeasts. It is slightly sweet, slightly sour, and slightly fizzy.

Natural carbonation comes from the carbon dioxide that yeasts make.

4. Health Benefits:

As a result of fermentation, substances like lactic acid and acetic acid are released into the drink. These acids make certain nutrients more available and create a slightly acidic environment that is good for gut health.

• The enzymes that are made during fermentation can help the digestive process.

5. Taking care of nature:

• The acids and alcohol that are made during fermentation lower the pH of the liquid. This makes a space where bad germs and molds can't grow, naturally keeping the drink fresh.

How to Take Care and Maintain Water Kefir Grains

1. Being fed:

• To keep grains healthy, they need to be fed sugar water on a daily basis. For constant fermentation, it's important to give them the right conditions and nutrients.

2. Storage:

• Water kefir grains can be kept in the fridge for short amounts of time in sugar water, or they can be dried and kept for a longer time. With the right care, they will stay alive and work well for future fermentations.

3. Revitalization:

• If grains get slow, cleaning them with clean water and giving them fresh sugar water can often wake them up. This can help get the microbes going again and get them fermenting again.

Chapter Six

Important Things You Need to Make Water Kefir

1. Jar of Glass

2. Non-Metallic Tools

3. Strainer made of plastic or wood

4. Measuring cups and spoons

5. Cloth or coffee filter that is clean

6. String or Rubber Band

7. Bottles that is clean to store

8. You can use a pH meter or pH strips.

9. Funnel(Not Required)

10. Clock or Timer

11. Towels or paper towels that are clean

12. Container for storing grains (not required)

13. Digital Scale (Not Required)

What You Need to Make Water Kefir

1. Water

- **Type:**

- Filtered water: This is the best because it is clean and doesn't contain chlorine or other chemicals that can stop fermentation.

- Another popular choice is coconut water, which gives you extra nutrients and a little taste.

Things to think about:

- Don't use distilled water because the kefir grains need nutrients that aren't in distilled water.

- Tap water is fine as long as it doesn't have any chlorine or chloramine in it. If it does, use a water filter or let it sit out for 24 hours to get rid of the chlorine.

2. Sugar

- **Type:**

- Organic cane sugar is what most people choose. For the kefir grains, it gives them a good mix of nutrients.

• Brown sugar: gives it a stronger taste and more minerals.

• Raw sugar is like cane sugar, but it hasn't been treated as much.

• Sucanat: higher mineral content cane sugar that has been treated less.

• **Quantity:**

• Basic Ratio: 1/4 to 1/2 cup of sugar for every quart (1 liter) of water. Change based on your personal taste and how active your grains are.

- Changing the Sugar: The amount of sugar you use may need to be changed based on the needs of your kefir grains and your personal taste.

Things to think about:

- Stay away from honey, sugar substitutes, and high-fructose corn syrup. These things can stop fermentation or hurt the grains.

3. Extra ingredients

- Flavorings:

- Fruits: During the second fermentation, you can add fresh or dried fruits for taste, such as berries, apple slices, figs, citrus slices, or citrus slices.

- Herbs: Spicy herbs like ginger, mint, or basil can give food a unique taste.

- Spices: To add more taste, you can use cinnamon sticks, cloves, or vanilla beans.

- **Juices:**

- Fruit Juices: During the second fermentation, adding a splash of fruit juice (like apple or lemon) can improve the taste and make the beer more carbonated.

- Stay away from juices that have extra sugars or preservatives.

- **Extra Nutritional Factors:**

- Mineral Addition: To increase the minerals, a small amount of sea salt or a mineral-rich salt (like Himalayan pink salt) can be used. This may be good for the kefir grains.

• Calcium: To help keep the kefir grains healthy, some recipes call for a small amount of calcium carbonate.

4. Alternatives to Sweeteners:

• Maple syrup: You can use a little of it, but it might change the color and taste.

• Agave Syrup: This is a less popular sweetener that you can use if you'd rather not use sugar.

...al rules for

...r the best fermentation, make sure the amount of sugar to water is just right. If you use too little sugar, the fermentation might not work well, and if you use too much, the kefir might be too sweet.

- Pure: To keep the brewing process going smoothly, use ingredients that are as pure as possible.

- Playing around: You can try out different flavors and seasonings to find the one that you like best.

Chapter Seven

Picking the Right Water: Why Water Quality Is Important

1. Purity and Composition

Filtered Water vs. Tap Water:

- **Filtered Water:** This type of water is best for making water kefir because it gets rid of chlorine, chloramine, and other chemicals that can stop the fermentation process. Activated carbon, reverse osmosis, and distilling are all types of filters.

- **Tap Water:** If you use tap water, make sure it doesn't have any chlorine or chloramine in it. The good bacteria in the kefir grains can be killed by chlorine, but chloramine stays in the grains longer and needs special treatments to get rid of.

- **Mineral Contents:**

- **Essential Minerals:** Calcium, magnesium, and potassium are some of the essential minerals that should be in the water. These minerals help the kefir grains stay healthy. The water that comes out of the tap and natural springs often has these minerals in it.

- **Distilled Water:** Distilled water doesn't have minerals that are needed for the kefir grains to work right and stay healthy.

2. Level of pH

• **Ideal pH:** To begin with, water should have a pH of 7. As acids are made during fermentation, the pH will drop. This helps keep the kefir fresh and stops dangerous bacteria from growing.

• **Monitoring:** If you use water that is very acidic or alkaline, it can change the brewing process. Making sure the starting pH is normal helps the fermentation process go smoothly and consistently.

3. Chlorine and Chloramine

• **Chlorine** is often added to city water to kill bacteria, but it can also hurt the good bacteria that are in kefir grains. Let water sit out in the open for 24 hours or use a water filter to get rid of chlorine.

• **Chloramine** is more solid than chlorine and doesn't break down as quickly. To get rid of chloramine in water, you need special filters.

4. Contaminant and Cleanliness

• **Contaminants:** Make sure the water doesn't have any heavy metals, pesticides, or other toxins in it. If the water is dirty, it can hurt the health of the kefir grains and lower the quality of the beverage.

- **Source:** Get clean, safe water from a source you can trust. If the tap water in your area isn't very good, natural spring water or mineral water in a bottle can be good options.

5. Water Temperature

- **Best temperature:** water should be at room temperature or a little warmer (68 to 75°F, 20 to 24°C). Kefir grains can be damaged or killed by very high or very low temperatures.

- **Don't heat:** If you use hot water from the tap, it can kill the live microorganisms in the kefir grains. Before you use the water, let it cool down to the right temperature.

6. Keeping up

• **Regular Use:** Using the same kind of water (filtered or bottled) every time can help keep fermentation results uniform. If the type or makeup of the water changes, it can affect the culturing process and the taste of the kefir.

Summary

Picking the right water is very important for making water kefir. Using filtered water that has the right amount of minerals and no dangerous chemicals will create a healthy environment for fermentation. This will lead to a tasty and healthy probiotic drink. To keep your kefir grains healthy and get the best results, you should always think about the pH, temperature, and quality of the water.

Chapter Eight

A Step-by-Step Guide How to Get Dried Water Kefir Grains

1. Get your stuff together.

• If you buy dried water kefir grains, make sure they come from a trustworthy source.

• Water that has been filtered: at room temperature or a little warmer.

• Organic cane sugar is best for use.

• Glass Jar Clean and won't respond.

• Spoon that isn't made of metal: plastic or wood.

- Cloth or coffee filter: to put over the jar.

- Rubber band or string: to keep the cover in place.

2. Get the sugar water ready.

- Mix Water and Sugar: Mix 1/4 cup (50 grams) of sugar with 1 quart (1 liter) of filtered water. Make sure to stir it well until the sugar is gone.

First, make sure the water is at room temperature, which is 68 to 75°F (20 to 24°C). Then, add the grains.

3. Wet the grains again.

- Add Grains to Water: Put the dried water kefir grains into the sugar water that has already been made. Make sure they are all submerged by gently stirring them.

• Soak the grains for 24 hours in the sugar water for the first step. Adding water to the grains during this time helps them come back to life and gets them ready for fermentation.

4. First fermentation

• Put the lid on the jar. Use a clean cloth or coffee filter to cover the top of the jar and connect it with a rubber band or string. This lets air move but keeps dirt and other things out.

- Let the jar sit at room temperature (68 to 75°F, 20 to 24°C) for 24 to 48 hours to ferment. The grains will start to work and grow at this point. As fermentation starts, you should see bubbles appear.

5. Observe the grains

- Do something: Check the grains after 24 hours. They should look full and stretchy, and there should be bubbling and a small change in the color of the water, which are all signs of fermentation.

- Taste Test: You can taste the water if you want to. A slightly sour taste should be present, which means fermentation has begun.

6. Rinse and move the grain

• Rinse Grains: After the first activation time, use a plastic or wooden strainer to gently remove the grains from the water. To get rid of any leftovers from when they were dry, rinse them under cool, filtered water.

• Make a New Batch: Add the rehydrated grains to a new batch of sugar water, making sure the sugar-to-water ratio is the same as the first batch. Fermentation will continue as usual.

7. Regular Maintance

• Feed the Grains: To keep them healthy and active, keep giving them fresh sugar water every 24 to 48 hours.

• Check and Make Changes: Look at the grains for signs of good fermentation. Based on how active the grains are, change the amount of sugar or the temperature of the water as needed.

8. How to Fix Problems

• Slow Fermentation: If fermentation is slow or not happening at all, make sure the water temperature is right and the grains have been rehydrated enough.

• Strange Smells or Tastes: If you notice strange tastes or smells, check to see if the water is contaminated or if there are problems with the sugar and water quality.

9. Long-Term Care:

• How to Store: If you need to stop making kefir, put the grains in sugar water and put them in the fridge. You can also dry them out and store them to keep them for a long time.

Chapter Nine

Simple Recipe: Step-by-Step Instructions for Making Water Kefir What You Need:

- 1/4 cup (50 grams) of sugar (cane sugar organic or other sugars that work)

- 1.25 liters of filtered water

- 2.25 to 3 tablespoons of water kefir grains that have been active and are ready to use

- If you want, you can add flavorings like fruit pieces, herbs, or spices for secondary fermentation.

Tools:

- A glass jar (at least a 1-quart size)
- Spoon made of plastic or wood
- Strainer made of plastic or wood
- Clothes or coffee filter (to cover the jar)
- Rubber band or string (to hold the cover in place)

Instruction:

1. Get the sugar water ready.

- Mix water and sugar: Mix 1/4 cup (50 grams) of sugar with 1 quart (1 liter) of filtered water in a clean glass jar. Mix the ingredients together until the sugar is gone. Before you add the grains, the water should be at room temperature, which is 68 to 75°F (20 to 24°C).

2. Add Water Kefir Grains:

• Add the grains slowly by adding two to three tablespoons of active water kefir grains to the jar of sugar water.

• Stir: Use a plastic or wooden spoon that isn't made of metal to gently stir the mixture so that the grains are spread out evenly.

3. Cover the Jar:

• Cover: Put a clean coffee filter or cloth over the top of the jar.

Use rubber band or rope to hold to hold tight. This lets air move but keeps dust and other things that aren't good out.

4. Let it ferment:

• Leave the jar at room temperature (68 to 75°F, 20 to 24°C) for 24 to 48 hours. The exact time will rely on how you like your food to taste and how active your grains are.

• Check: Bubbles should start to form during fermentation, and the water may start to taste a little sour. After 24 hours, you can try a taste to see if you like it.

5. Strain the Kefir

• As the fermentation process is over, use a plastic or wooden sieve to separate the water kefir grains from the liquid. Move the grains to a clean jar or bowl so they can be used again.

• Rinse the grains. If you want to get rid of any leftovers, you can gently rinse the grains with cool, filtered water before starting a new batch.

6. Put the kefir in bottles

• Move: Put the fermented water kefir into clean bottles to store it. Add fruit pieces, herbs, or spices now if you want to make it taste better.

• Seal: Put sealed caps on the bottles to close them up. If you added flavorings, you can let them ferment for another 24 hours (secondary fermentation) to make the taste stronger and the carbonation higher.

7. Store

• Put in the fridge: Put the bottled water kefir in the fridge. It can be eaten in one to two weeks. It's best to drink the kefir as soon as possible because it will continue to ferment slowly in the fridge.

8. Make a fresh batch

• For a new batch of water kefir, start by adding the grains that were filtered to a new batch of sugar water. Repeat

Optional: Second-stage fermentation

• **Flavoring:** To add more taste, put herbs (like mint) or fruits (like berries or citrus) in the bottles before you seal them. This step also makes the carbonation stronger.

• **Ferment:** Let the sweetened kefir sit at room temperature for another 24 hours to ferment.

Enjoy after putting it in the fridge to stop the ripening.

Chapter Ten

Adding flavor to your water kefir: Adding herbs, fruits, and other tastes

1. Some basic rules for flavoring

• When to add the flavors: after the first fermentation of the water kefir, during the secondary fermentation process.

• For every quart (1 liter) of water kefir, add about 1/4 to 1/2 cup of fruit or other flavorings. Change based on your personal taste.

• Fruits, herbs, and spices can be used whether they are fresh, frozen, or dried. Make sure they are clean and don't have any extra ingredients or chemicals.

2. Adding Fruits:

• New Fruits: If you want to eat berries (strawberries, blueberries, raspberries), citrus fruits (lemons, limes, oranges), apples, or pears, you can slice or chop them. Put it right into the kefir bottles.

•Fruits that are frozen can be put right away without having to be thawed first. Most of the time, they give off more color and taste.

• Dried fruits: Don't use too many because they are very concentrated. Fruits like raisins, figs, and dates are examples. If the dried fruits are very hard, soak them in water before adding them to the kefir.

3. Putting Herbs in It:

• Fresh Herbs: Put in fresh herbs like rosemary, basil, or mint. Before you add the herbs, lightly crush them to get the oils out.

• Dried Herbs: Don't use too many dried herbs because they can make the tastes too strong. Dried lavender or chamomile are two examples.

4. Adding Spices:

• Whole Spices: Put in whole spices like star anise, cinnamon sticks, or cloves. These should only be added in small amounts, and they can be taken out after the dressing is done.

• Ground Spices: Use small amounts of ground spices like ginger and nutmeg. They might settle to the bottom of the bottle if you don't shake it first.

5. Putting in flavorings and extracts

• Vanilla Extract: Just a few drops of pure vanilla extract can make something smell and taste great.

- Citrus Zest: Zest from lemon, lime, or orange can make the citrus taste stronger without making it too sweet.

6. The Process of Flavoring

1. Get the flavorings ready by:

- Wash and Cut: Clean fresh herbs, spices, and veggies and get them ready to use. If you need to, chop or slice.

- Measure: Use a measuring cup to get the amount of flavoring items you want.

2. Fill up with bottles:

- Transfer Kefir: Once the first fermentation is done, pour the water kefir into clean bottles, making sure there is some space at the top.

• Add Flavorings: Put the already-cooked herbs, spices, or fruits into the bottles.

3. Seal and Keep the ferment:

• Seal the Bottles: Put caps on the bottles and close them tightly. Adding gas during secondary fermentation is helped by this.

• For the second fermentation, leave the bottles out in the open air for 24 hours. The flavorings will mix with the kefir, and bubbles will start to form.

4 Refrigerate:

- Chill: Once the second fermentation is done, put the flavored kefir in the fridge to stop the fermentation process and enjoy it cold.

5. Strain before drinking (optional):

- Get rid of flavors: You can strain out big chunks of fruit or herbs before drinking if you'd like.

7. Trying Out Different Flavors

- Make Blends: Try mixing fruits, herbs, and spices in different ways to find new and tasty tastes.

- Seasonal Changes: To make your water kefir more interesting and fresh, use fruits and herbs that are in season.

Classic Tastes: Recipes for Classic Water Kefir Drinks

1. Kefir with lemon and ginger

Ingredients

- 1 quart (1 liter) of water kefir,

- 1 to 2 lemon slices (or 1to 2 tablespoons of fresh lemon juice),

- 1to 2 teaspoons of fresh grated ginger (or half a teaspoon of dried ginger

- For extra sweetness, you can add 1 to 2 tablespoons of honey or maple syrup.

Instruction:

1. Get the kefir ready. Once the first fermentation is done, pour the water kefir into a clean glass bottle, making sure there is some room at the top.

2. Change the taste: Put the lemon slices and newly grated ginger into the bottle. Add the honey or maple syrup now if you're using it.

3. Seal and Ferment: Put a tight lid on the bottle and leave it at room temperature for 24 hours to

allow secondary fermentation to happen.

4. Put in the fridge: Put the kefir in the fridge to cool it down before drinking it. If you want, you can strain out the ginger and lemon pieces.

2. Berry Blast Kefir Water

- One quart (1 liter) of water kefir;
- half a cup of mixed berries, like blackberries, raspberries, strawberries, or blueberries
- And, if you want, one to two tablespoons of honey or agave syrup for sweetness.

Instruction:

1. Get Kefir Ready: Once the first fermentation is done, moves the water kefir to a clean glass bottle.

2. Add tastes: Put the mixed berries in the bottle. Adding sweets is also important.

3. put the lid on the bottle and let it sit at room temperature for 24 hours.

4. Refrigerate: Once the kefir has been sweetened, put it in the fridge. You can strain the berries out if you'd like.

Orange and mint water kefir:

•1 quart (1 liter) of water kefir,

- 1 to 2 slices of orange or lime,

- Handful of fresh mint leaves,

- 1 to 2 drops of honey or agave syrup.

Guidelines:

1. Get the kefir ready by putting the water kefir into a clean glass bottle.

2. Add Flavorings: Add the mint leaves and citrus pieces. If you're using sugars, put them in now.

3 seal the bottle and let it ferment. After 24 hours at room temperature, seal the bottle and let it ferment again.

4. Put the kefir in the fridge. If you want, you can strain out the mint and citrus before eating.

Apple Cinnamon Water Kefir:

- 1quart (1 liter) of water kefir

- A half-apple, sliced thinly

- A cinnamon stick (or half teaspoon of ground cinnamon)

- 1-2 tablespoons of maple syrup, if you want it sweeter

Instruction:

1: Make the kefir. Pour the water kefir into a clean glass bottle after the first fermenting.

2. Add Flavorings: Put the apple slices and cinnamon stick (or

ground cinnamon) into the bottle. Put in the maple syrup now if you're using it.

3. Seal and Ferment: Put a tight lid on the bottle and turn it upside down for 24 hours.

4. Put in the fridge: Once you're happy with the taste, put the kefir in the fridge. If you'd rather, you can strain out the apple pieces and cinnamon stick before drinking.

5. Pineapple Coconut Water Kefir:

- 1 quart (1 liter) of water kefir
- 2 cups of pineapple chunks
- 1/4 cup of shredded coconut

• For extra sweetness, you can add 1 to 2 tablespoons of honey or agave syrup.

How to Do It:

1. Get Kefir ready: Fill a clean glass bottle with the water kefir.

2. Add Flavorings: Add the coconut shreds and pineapple chunks. Adding sweets is also important.

3. seal the bottle and let it ferment. After 24 hours at room temperature, seal the bottle and let it ferment again.

4. Put the kefir in the fridge. If you want, strain out the

pineapple chunks and coconut after chilling.

How to Get the Classic Flavors

• Try it out: You can change how much of the fruits, herbs, and spices you use to your liking.

• Freshness: For the best taste and health benefits, use fresh products.

Carbonation: If you want more carbonation, leave the bottles out at room temperature for a little longer before putting them in the fridge.

How to Store and Keep Kefir Fresh

1. Refrigeration

• Storage: Put your water kefir in the fridge after the brewing process is done. It helps to slow down the fermentation process so that the taste and quality of the kefir are kept.

• Containers: To keep the carbonation from escaping and the drink from getting dirty, use glass or plastic bottles with tight-fitting caps or lids.

• Shelf Life: Water kefir can stay fresh in the fridge for one to two weeks if it is stored properly. The taste might change more over time, and it might get tangier.

2. Freezing up

- Purpose: Water kefir can be kept fresh for longer by freezing it. Keep in mind that freezing kefir can change its structure and taste, so it's best to save it for a long time.

- Steps: Pour the kefir into containers that can go in the freezer, leaving room at the top for it to expand. Label with the date and a tight seal.

- Shelf Life: You can freeze water kefir for three to six months. To use, let it thaw in the fridge and give it a good shake to mix.

3. Storing Kefir Grains for a Long Time

- If you need to stop making kefir, put the grains in a jar with sugar water and put it in the fridge. To keep the oats healthy, change the sugar water every one to two weeks.

- Drying: To keep kefir grains for a long time, rinse them with cool water, pat them dry, and put them in a jar with a little sugar that can be sealed. Keep it somewhere cool and dark. By following the reheating process, dried grains can be used again later.

4. Handling and Safety

• Cleanliness: To keep things from getting contaminated, always use clean containers and tools. Do not use metal containers or tools with the kefir because they can react with it and hurt the grains.

• To avoid cross-contamination, store kefir away from raw meats, unwashed fruits and vegetables, and other foods that could be harmful in the fridge.

5. Checking the Quality:

• Taste and Smell: Check the kefir often for any off tastes or smells that you don't like. A little sour is fine, but sour or spoiled smells mean the kefir may be past its best.

• Visual Inspection: Look for mold or cloudiness that doesn't make sense. If there is mold on the kefir, throw it away and clean the jar well before making another batch.

6. Tips for Keeping Things Fresh

• Put in fresh ingredients: If you want the best results and a longer shelf life, start with fresh, high-quality products.

• Batch Size: If you can't finish the kefir in the time it says to, you might want to make smaller amounts. This way, you'll always have fresh yogurt on hand.

7. Extra Space for Fermentation

• Put in the fridge right away: If you added flavors during secondary fermentation, put the kefir in the fridge as soon as the taste and carbonation are just right.

• Keep an eye on carbonation: Bottles can pop if they have too much carbonation. Be careful, and if the bottles get too fizzy, you might want to "burp" them, which means opening them quickly to let out extra pressure.